I0813182

ENGINEERING ANSWERS

How Dams Hold Back Water

BY MARNE VENTURA

Kids Core
An Imprint of Abdo Publishing
abdobooks.com

abdobooks.com

Printed in the United States of America, North Mankato, Minnesota.
102024
012025

Cover Photo: Leonid Andronov/Shutterstock Images
Interior Photos: Shutterstock Images, 4–5, 20–21, 24, 29 (bottom); Sean Pavone/Shutterstock Images, 6; Dominic Gentilcore, PhD/Shutterstock Images, 9; Paulo Benedetto/Shutterstock Images, 10; Mateusz Lopuszynski/Shutterstock Images, 12–13; T. Schofield/Shutterstock Images, 14; Nadia Yong/Shutterstock Images, 17; Zern Liew/Shutterstock Images, 18 (top left), 18 (top right), 18 (bottom left), 18 (bottom right); Josh Edelson/AFP/Getty Images, 23; Mike Seaman/Shutterstock Images, 25; Matt T. Jackson/Shutterstock Images, 26; Jose Luis Stephens/Shutterstock Images, 28; Andrey Shchekalev/Shutterstock Images, 29 (top)

Editor: Marley Richmond
Series Designer: Laura Kuchar

Library of Congress Control Number: 2024938376

Publisher's Cataloging-in-Publication Data

Names: Ventura, Marne, author.
Title: How dams hold back water / by Marne Ventura
Description: Minneapolis, Minnesota: ABDO Publishing, 2025 | Series: Engineering answers | Includes online resources and index.
Identifiers: ISBN 9781098295868 (lib. bdg.) | ISBN 9798384916864 (ebook)
Subjects: LCSH: Engineering--Juvenile literature. | Dams--Juvenile literature. | Flood dams and reservoirs--Juvenile literature. | Design-build process (Construction industry)--Juvenile literature. | Questions and answers--Juvenile literature. | Engineering design--Juvenile literature.
Classification: DDC 620.1--dc23

CONTENTS

CHAPTER 1
An Engineering Marvel 4

CHAPTER 2
Types of Dams 12

CHAPTER 3
How Dams Control Floods 20

Engineering Facts 28
Glossary 30
Online Resources 31
Learn More 31
Index 32
About the Author 32

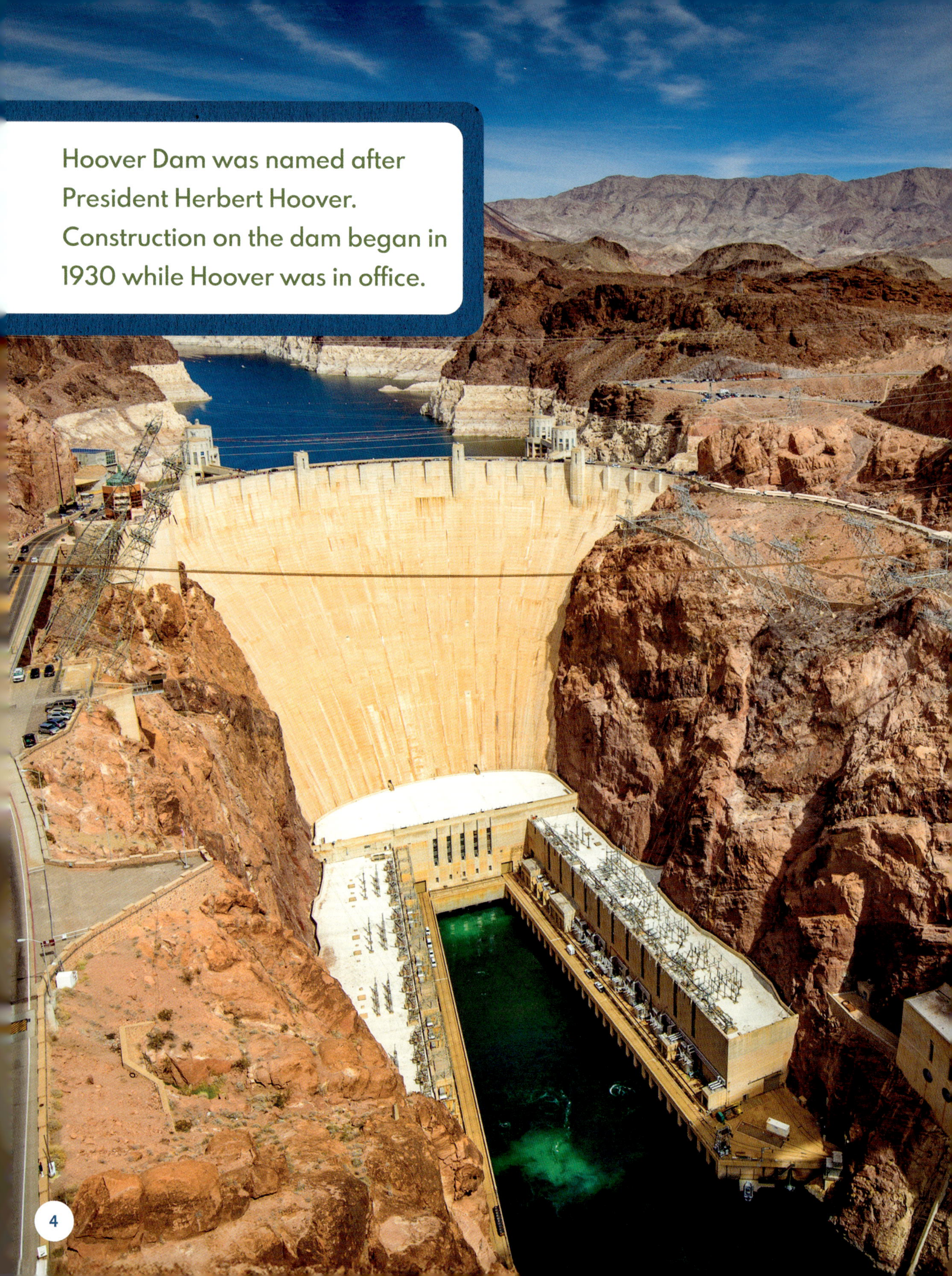

Hoover Dam was named after President Herbert Hoover. Construction on the dam began in 1930 while Hoover was in office.

CHAPTER 1

An Engineering Marvel

Caden stood on a bridge walkway. He was on the **crest** of Hoover Dam. He looked down at a huge wall of concrete. "It's so big!" he said.

Caden was on a school field trip to Hoover Dam. The tour guide spoke to the class.

There are 17 large generators in Hoover Dam's power plant. Each year, these machines produce enough electricity to meet the needs of 1.3 million people.

"Hoover Dam stands 726 feet, or 222 meters, high. That is as tall as a 60-story building," she said. She explained that the dam stretches between the sides of the Black Canyon. It is on the border of Arizona and Nevada.

Hoover Dam holds back the water of the Colorado River. The water it blocks forms Lake Mead. This is the largest human-made lake in the United States.

"What's at the bottom?" asked Caden. He was looking **downstream**.

"The building at the base of the dam on the downstream side is a power plant," the tour guide said. "Waterpower is made into electricity there."

Caden and his classmates were surprised by the dam's size. The tour guide said the dam was completed in 1935. At that time, it was the tallest dam in the world.

She explained, "Its base is the thickness of two football fields, end to end. The concrete used to build the dam would pave a road from San Francisco to New York City." The class continued walking. They were ready to learn more about how Hoover Dam works.

What Is a Dam?

Dams are some of the largest structures ever built. Dams stretch across streams

Hoover Dam Today

People in Nevada, Arizona, and California depend on the Hoover Dam. It **irrigates** more than 1.5 million acres (607,000 ha) of land. It provides water to more than 16 million people. Power made by the dam provides energy to more than 500,000 homes.

People work to build dams that do not harm the environment. Some dams have fish ladders that allow fish to swim upriver and pass through the dam.

or rivers. Dams stop some water from running downstream. Many dams help keep rivers from flooding.

Water builds up behind a dam. It creates a lake called a reservoir. Homes, businesses, and farms use water from reservoirs. People fish and boat on them too.

Beavers create natural dams out of sticks, trees, and mud. These dams control the flow of rivers too.

People have built dams for thousands of years. Today, **engineers** design dams to control and use the power of water. Dams make the surrounding land safe and useful for people.

Primary Source

President Theodore Roosevelt passed an act to pay for dams in the American West in 1902. This area is dry, so water from dams' reservoirs could water crops. He said:

> One hundred and sixty acres [65 ha] of fairly rich and well-watered soil . . . may keep a family in plenty, whereas no one could get a living out of 160 acres of dry pasture land.

Source: "The Arid West." *Theodore Roosevelt Center Blog*, 17 June 2013, theodorerooseveltcenter.org. Accessed 18 Mar. 2024.

What's the Big Idea?

Read this quote carefully. What is its main idea? Explain how the main idea is supported by details.

Engineers think about the size, shape, and strength of a river when deciding on the type and location of a new dam.

Types of Dams

All dams control the flow of water. They are built of earth, rock, or concrete. Types of dams hold back water in different ways. The most common types are embankment, gravity, arch, and buttress dams.

The W.A.C. Bennett Dam is a large embankment dam in Canada.

Embankment and Gravity Dams

Most dams in the United States are embankment dams. They are made of soil and rock. A layer of clay or cement is sometimes added. This layer stops leaks through gaps between rocks.

The strongest **force** pushing against a dam is water flowing down the river. This is called water pressure. Water pressure is stronger at the bottom of the river than on the surface. Engineers build embankment dams to be wider at the bottom than at the top. Both sides of the dam slope outward from the top. The thick bottom can stand up to stronger pressure.

How Dams Are Built

To build dams, workers need a dry area. They have to divert the river. They direct the water to flow somewhere else. Once the site is dry, workers lay the foundation. This is the base of the dam. The heavier the dam, the stronger and deeper the foundation needs to be.

An embankment dam is heavy. The weight pushes into the bottom of the river. This makes the dam strong. The dam is heavy enough to push back against the force of the river.

Gravity dams are made of concrete. They are usually much larger than embankment dams. Gravity dams often have one side that is straight up and down. The other side slopes out. Similar to embankment dams, gravity dams hold up to the force of water with their weight. These dams are also widest at the bottom.

Arch and Buttress Dams

Arch dams are also made of concrete. These types of dams are curved on the **upstream** side. Flowing water pushes against the curve.

Either side of a gravity dam can be sloped. The Grand Coulee Dam in Washington is a gravity dam. Its slope is on the downriver side.

Types of Dams

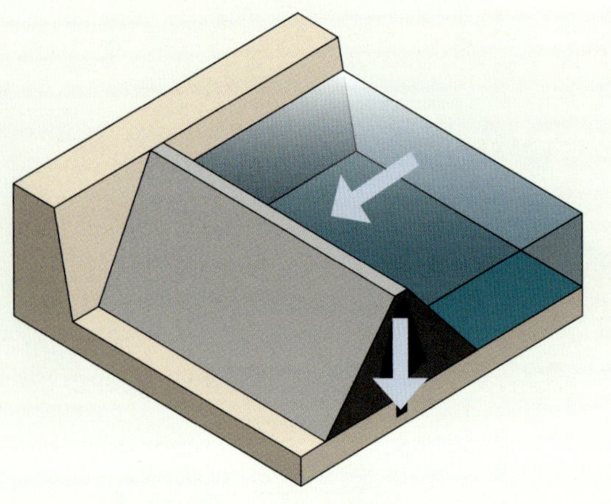

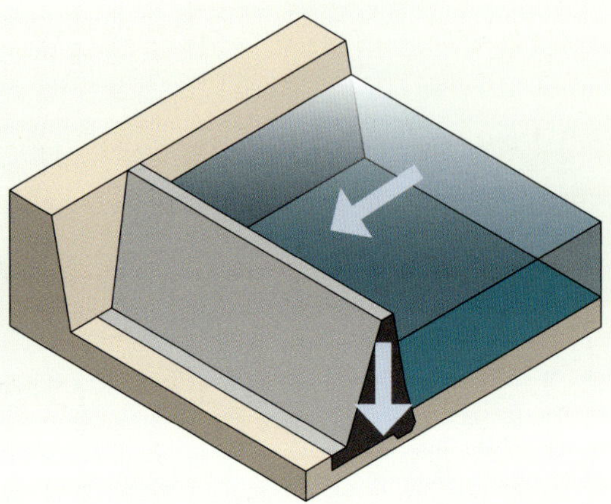

Arch dam

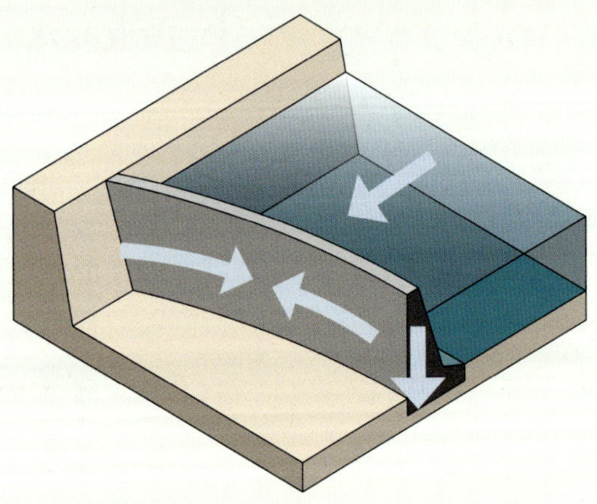

Buttress dam

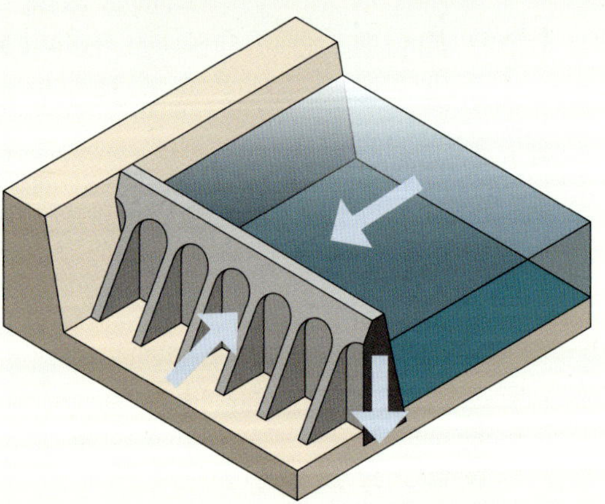

Dams are built to stand up to the force of water. Each type of dam handles that force in a different way.

This causes the curve to compress. This means the concrete is pushed inward. It forms a tighter curve. This makes the dam even stronger. Hoover Dam is an arch-gravity dam. It uses elements from both types of dams.

Buttress dams have concrete supports, or buttresses, on the downstream side. The water flow pushes against the dam from upstream. The buttresses push back and support the dam.

Further Evidence

Look at the website below. Does it give any new evidence to support Chapter Two?

All About Dams

abdocorelibrary.com/dams-hold-back-water

Engineers sometimes design dams to protect areas that have flooded in the past.

CHAPTER 3

How Dams Control Floods

Water from rain and melting snow runs into rivers and streams. Some water flows downstream. Soil under the river **absorbs** water too. At times, water enters a river faster than the river can absorb it or carry it away. This causes a flood.

The water level rises higher than the riverbank, and the river overflows.

Floods can damage roads and buildings. They can injure people and wildlife. In the United States, 90 percent of natural disasters involve floods.

Slowing the Flow

Dams reduce the risk of floods by controlling the flow of water. When water levels rise, dams push more water into their reservoirs. But wet weather might cause the reservoir to rise too high. Then, water flows into spillways.

Spillways are passages for water. Many spillways lead over or around the dam wall. They stop water from flowing over the crest.

Dams may fail during heavy rain if they are not designed to handle extra water.

Many spillways are concrete channels. Some are open paths with sidewalls. Others are tunnels through the ground.

This could damage the dam. Spillways often lead back to the river. Long spillways give the rushing water a chance to slow down. This reduces possible damage to the river. It also gives soil time to absorb more water.

Water leaving a spillway may be rough and swirling. If it is too strong, this water can damage the ground around and under the river.

Extra water can also pass through openings in dams called sluice gates or slide gates. These gates are often built into dam walls.

Hydroelectricity

Moving water is powerful. Some dams turn waterpower into electricity. This is called hydroelectricity. Pipes in the dam move flowing water to a power plant. The water turns wheels called turbines. The turbines run generators. These machines produce electricity.

Sluice gates allow water to pass through the dam without damaging the crest of the dam.

They can be opened or closed. Workers can control how much water passes through the dam by opening or closing the gates.

About 90,000 dams play an important role in US life. The electricity produced by dams is **renewable energy**. Just 2,300 dams make about 30 percent of the renewable energy in the United States. Dams are some of the most amazing structures in the world. They are a symbol of how humans use engineering to harness the power of nature.

Explore Online

Visit the website below. Does it give any information about dams that was not in Chapter Three?

Dams

abdocorelibrary.com/dams-hold-back-water

Engineering Facts

Reservoirs hold extra water that may be used by businesses, homes, and farms.

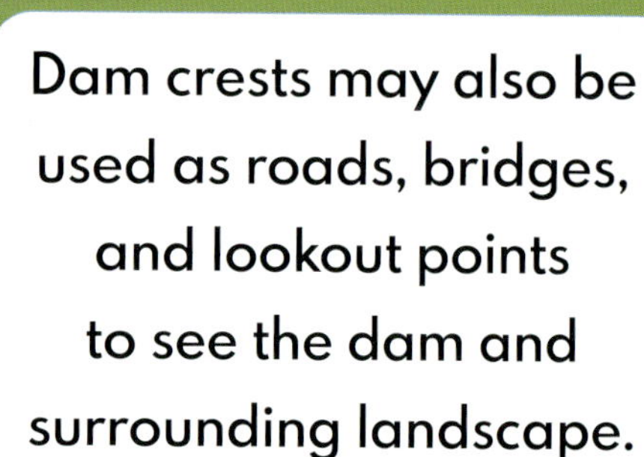

Dam crests may also be used as roads, bridges, and lookout points to see the dam and surrounding landscape.

Dam power plants turn waterpower into electricity.

Spillways are pathways for extra water if a dam's reservoir is full.

Glossary

absorb
to take in something such as water

crest
the top of a dam wall

downstream
toward the direction the river flows

engineers
people who are trained to design and build machines and structures

force
a push or pull that transfers energy into an object

irrigates
supplies with water for crops

renewable energy
energy that is made from a source that can't be used up, such as waterpower

upstream
the opposite direction the river flows

Online Resources

To learn more about dams, visit our free resource websites below.

Visit **abdocorelibrary.com** or scan this QR code for free Common Core resources for teachers and students, including vetted activities, multimedia, and booklinks, for deeper subject comprehension.

Visit **abdobooklinks.com** or scan this QR code for free additional online weblinks for further learning. These links are routinely monitored and updated to provide the most current information available.

Learn More

Garré, Sarah, and Marijke Huysmans. *The Wonderful World of Water: From Dams to Deserts.* Prestel, 2023.

Mattern, Joanne. *How Bridges Stand Strong.* Abdo, 2025.

Index

arch dams, 13, 16–19

buttress dams, 13, 18, 19

compression, 19

embankment dams, 13–16, 18
engineers, 10, 15

flooding, 9, 21–22
foundations, 15

gravity dams, 13, 16–19

Hoover Dam, 5–8, 19

power plants, 7, 25

renewable energy, 27
reservoirs, 9, 11, 22

sluice gate, 25–26
spillways, 22–24

water pressure, 15

About the Author

Marne Ventura is the author of more than 150 books for children. She holds a master's degree in education from the University of California. She enjoys writing about STEM, arts and crafts, finance, people and places, food, and careers. Ventura and her family live in California.